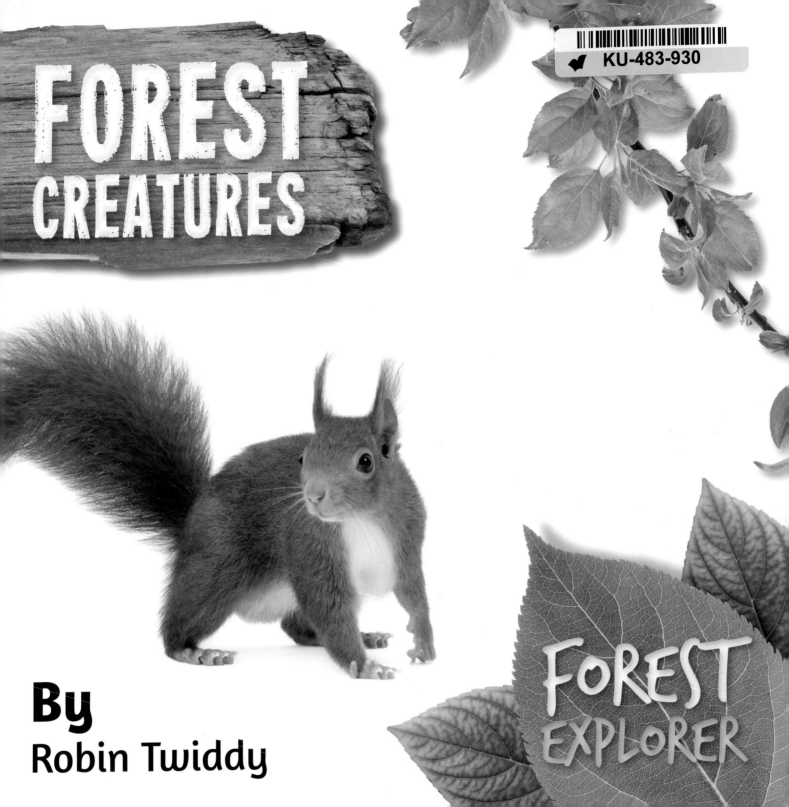

FOREST CREATURES

By
Robin Twiddy

FOREST
EXPLORER

BookLife
PUBLISHING

©2018
BookLife Publishing
King's Lynn
Norfolk PE30 4LS
All rights reserved.
Printed in Malaysia.

ISBN: 978-1-78637-475-2

Written by:
Robin Twiddy

Edited by:
Kirsty Holmes

Designed by:
Gareth Liddington

CONTENTS

LET'S EXPLORE

WELCOME, FOREST EXPLORER!
Today we will be looking for forest creatures. We will learn about some of the animals that live in the forest.

GRAB YOUR EQUIPMENT

A budding forest explorer will need:

Camera

Binoculars

Notebook

Walking Boots

DIFFERENT ANIMALS

There are lots of different creatures that live in the forest. Depending on where you live, you will find different animals.

Red deer can be found in lots of forests all around the world.

Make sure you have an adult explorer with you.

We should always be careful exploring the forest. Some animals can be dangerous if they are **startled**. So try not to make too much noise.

BIG CREATURES

Pandas are found in the forests of China. They are very shy!

Big creatures such as deer, bears or badgers can be found in different forests around the world. Which large animals live in the forest near you?

Big animals leave bigger droppings that are easier to find. Fresh animal poo means that the creature is probably still nearby.

Fox droppings with berries.

YOU CAN TELL A LOT ABOUT AN ANIMAL FROM ITS DROPPINGS, BUT DON'T TOUCH!

SMALL CREATURES

Small creatures can be hard to see in the forest.
If you are quiet and look carefully you might find:

Mouse

Bat

Squirrel

Stoat

...and lots more!

Mice have poor eyesight but very good hearing.

Mice are part of the rodent family. Most mice are **nocturnal** creatures. They have round ears and a long tail. Mice eat fruit and grains.

11

TREE-DWELLING CREATURES

Pine Marten

When exploring the forest you should try looking up!
Lots of forest creatures are **tree-dwellers**. You might find
monkeys, rodents or **felines** up there.

Squirrels can be found in most forests because they are tree-dwelling animals. They have bushy tails and eat nuts and seeds.

Squirrels bury nuts to save them for the winter.

WATER

A good place to look for animals is near water. Creatures go to streams to drink and look for food.

Some animals live in, or near the water.

Amphibians are born in water, then slowly change so they can live on land.

Amphibians are animals that live both in and out of the water. These include toads, frogs and salamanders. Amphibians mostly eat insects and spiders.

The koala can be found in the forests of Australia.

Some forest creatures are **herbivores** and some are **carnivores**. There is lots to eat in the forest if you are a herbivore.

Some forest animals are hunters. They eat other animals that are **prey**. Some forest hunters are:

Hedgehog

Shrew

Fox

Wolf

Predators come in all shapes and sizes.

LOOKING FOR SIGNS

Keep an eye out for signs that forest creatures have been nearby. Look for places that animals could take shelter, such as hollow trees.

Racoons

Make sure not to disturb any animals living there.

Herbivores can be found in parts of the forest with lots of plants and good places to hide. So look for thick bushes and big rocks.

WATCHING ANIMALS

Remember that the creatures of the forest are not pets.
Use your binoculars to watch them from a distance.
Try not to make any noise!

The best time to see animals in the forest is either early in the morning or in the evening before the sun sets.

Keep a record of the animals you see.

KEEPING NOTES

When you do see animals while exploring, it is important to keep careful notes. This way you will be able to **identify** them later.

Animal: Adult Deer
Size: large
Colour: Brown
Eats: Leaves

Note what it looked like and what it was doing.

If you have a camera with you, take some photographs
to add to your notebook.

GLOSSARY

carnivores	animals that eat other animals rather than plants
felines	animals of the cat family
herbivores	animals that only eat plants
identify	spot or recognise
nocturnal	active at night instead of during the day
predators	animals that hunt other animals for food
prey	animals that are hunted by other animals for food
startled	frightened and surprised
tree-dwellers	animals that live in trees

INDEX